THE APPLE EFFECT

CORE BUSINESS STRATEGIES FOR SCALING GROWTH

APPLE LEVY

The Apple Effect: CORE Business Strategies for Scaling Growth

Copyright © 2025 Apple Levy All rights reserved.

No part of this publication may be reproduced, distributed, or transmitted in any form or by any means, including photocopying, recording, or other electronic or mechanical methods, without the prior written permission of the publisher, except in the case of brief quotations embodied in critical reviews and certain other noncommercial uses permitted by copyright law.

For permission requests, please contact:
Apple Levy
www.AppleLevy.com
hello@applelevy.com

First Edition
ISBN (Paperback): 979-8-9990484-1-7
ISBN (Hardcover): 979-8-9990484-0-0
ISBN (eBook): 979-8-9990484-2-4

Cover and interior design by Apple Levy
Printed in the United States of America

CONTENTS

Acknowledgments	V
Why This Book Can't Wait	X
Introduction to The Apple Effect A Business Built to Scale	XII
1. Building High-Performing Teams The Core of Growth	2
2. Creating Accountability & Ownership at Every Level Own the Outcome or Own the Excuse	17
3. Apples & Oranges Why Copying What Works for Others Can Break What You're Building	31
4. KPI Mastery Turning Data into Scalable Decisions	44
5. The Growth Mindset Scaling Beyond Comfort Zones	59

6. Mastering OKRs & Performance Alignment Clarity. Focus. Momentum.	74
7. Mastering Leadership Leading for Growth & Scale	90
8. Precision Execution Turning Action into Momentum	104
The C.O.R.E. Strategy Engine Engineered to Scale. Built to Last.	118
The Whole: Wrapping It All Together Building a Legacy Business	131
Bonus Resource: The C.O.R.E Kit Tech & Templates to Implement Faster	138
About the Author	146
Let's Take The Apple Effect Off the Page and Into Your Business	149

ACKNOWLEDGMENTS

This book began as a conversation, an idea shared over a notepad, a question asked over a phone call, a nudge from someone who saw what I couldn't yet articulate.

AL Simpson, thank you for lighting that spark. You gave this book its name, its bones, and the belief that I could actually do this. You saw the book before I did and made me see it, too.

Bill Wilson, you've been a steady voice in my corner, pushing me not to settle, not to shrink, and not to stop. Your mentorship is woven into more than just these pages; it's in the way I lead, speak, and show up.

To my friend and PM consultant - thank you for the three months of deep dives, the hours of problem-solving, and the conversation that turned into Slice 3. Your fingerprints are all over the practical side of this work.

To my clients - you are the reason this book exists. Your challenges, your breakthroughs, your grit. Every one of you sharpened the strategies in this book. These aren't abstract ideas. They're the result of showing up, side by side, and doing the real work.

To my husband, Damon - you've always been my biggest fan and the loudest supporter of my wildest dreams. Thank you for seeing the future with me.

And to my daughter, Sabrina - you are my why. I write, lead, and live out loud so you'll always know what's possible when you stay bold, stay kind, and bet on yourself.

ACKNOWLEDGING THE GIANTS BEHIND THE GROWTH

Behind every meaningful transformation are the voices, hands, and hearts that guided it. These are two of mine.

ALBERT SIMPSON - ENTREPRENEUR | CEO COACH | EXIT STRATEGY CONSULTANT

Albert Simpson is a veteran entrepreneur, coach, and advisor with over 20 years of experience building, scaling, and successfully exiting technology companies. He has co-founded and led multiple ventures, including IPM.domains (acquired by CentralNic) and eBrandSecure (acquired by CSC), serving Fortune 1000 and FTSE-listed companies across the globe.

Albert specializes in helping founders prepare their businesses for high-value exits. His consulting focuses on operational optimization, financial clarity, and strategic positioning, ensuring companies are structurally sound and market-ready when it's time to sell.

With a strong background in executive leadership (CEO, COO, CRO), he brings a hands-on, strategic approach to scaling teams, driving profitability, and navigating complex M&A processes. Albert has worked on both sides of the table and knows what acquirers look for and how to deliver it.

AREAS OF EXPERTISE:

- Growth & Scale Strategy
- M&A Readiness & Exit Planning
- Revenue Optimization & Operational Efficiency
- Team Structuring & Executive Leadership
- Strategic Partnerships & Buy-Side Relationships
- Due Diligence Preparation (Legal, Financial,

Operational)

Whether you're growing toward acquisition or just starting to think about the next chapter, Albert provides actionable insights and practical support to help you build a company worth buying.

BILL WILSON - ENTREPRENEUR | CEO/COO/CFO COACH | FINANCIAL AND OPERATIONAL STRATEGY CONSULTANT

Bill Wilson is a seasoned entrepreneur and executive coach with over 25 years of experience in driving operational excellence and financial performance across diverse industries. Having held pivotal roles such as CEO, CFO, and COO, he brings a rare combination of strategic vision and hands-on leadership that consistently delivers revenue growth and sustainable business transformation.

Bill has an exceptional ability to identify growth opportunities, streamline operations, and implement financial strategies that enhance profitability. His areas of expertise include budgeting, forecasting, M&A, and organizational restructuring, making him an invaluable partner for companies navigating complexity and scale.

He has founded and led multiple successful ventures, building high-performing teams and fostering cultures of accountability and innovation. His leadership style blends discipline with empathy, and his coaching consistently earns the trust of C-suite executives.

Bill also served as a first-year mentor in the USC Marshall School of Business Entrepreneur MBA Program, where he coached students on refining and launching future business ventures. He currently serves on the Board of Directors for Eloquence Communications, Inc.

Today, Bill continues to guide executives through critical inflection points, bringing clarity, stability, and long-term strategy to the table.

WHY THIS BOOK CAN'T WAIT

You didn't pick up this book because everything was running perfectly.

You picked it up because something feels off.
Maybe your team isn't executing.
Maybe your margins are shrinking.
Maybe you're stuck doing everything yourself again.
Or maybe you've grown fast… but not on purpose.

And now you're asking:

Can this business keep scaling, or is it going to collapse under the weight of my own success?

Let's get aligned: **This book isn't theory.**

And it's not written for people who are "fine" maintaining the status quo.

This book is a wake-up call.

It's for the founder who's tired of being the bottleneck.

The operator who's ready to stop reacting.

The leader who's done settling for chaos disguised as growth.

Because here's what most people won't say out loud:

Energy doesn't scale. Systems do.

If your business only works when you are in the room, you don't have a business.

You have a job.

A stressful one. A self-made one. But a job nonetheless.

You deserve better. And your business is capable of more.

That's what *The Apple Effect* delivers: a repeatable system for creating clarity, duplicating leadership, and scaling with precision, on your terms.

No feel-good nonsense. Just the frameworks, insights, and proof I've used to help real business owners transform from overworked operators into high-impact architects.

This book can't wait, because your team can't keep waiting. Your margins won't fix themselves. And your vision deserves structure, not just hustle.

Let's get to work - *Apple*

INTRODUCTION TO THE APPLE EFFECT

A Business Built to Scale

I know you didn't start your business just to stay stuck in the weeds, putting out fires, chasing down missed deadlines, or answering the same question five different ways. You started it because you had a vision. A product. A service. A problem worth solving. And in the beginning, your energy alone was enough to carry it forward.

But energy doesn't scale. Systems do.

Most businesses don't fail because of bad ideas or lack of hustle. They fail because the owner becomes the bottleneck.

At some point, the growth you worked so hard to create starts breaking the business you built. You hit a ceiling, not because you lack drive, but because your structure wasn't built for the scale you're aiming for.

That's where *The Apple Effect* comes in.

WHAT IS THE APPLE EFFECT?

This book is a framework I've used in the real world with real business owners across multiple industries. It's the structure behind sustainable growth and high-performance teams.

Think of it like slicing open an apple. Each slice reveals a part of the whole: a core principle that, when executed intentionally, gives your business the clarity, control, and confidence to scale.

THE C.O.R.E. FRAMEWORK

- **Culture** – Build a high-performing, aligned, and accountable team.

- **Operational Excellence** – Create systems that make success repeatable.

- **Results & Accountability** – Measure what matters and empower ownership.

- **Expansion & Innovation** – Multiply your impact and stay ahead of the curve.

This isn't about fixing everything overnight. It's about sequencing the right moves, in the right order, with the right strategy to actually win.

Each chapter in this book is a "slice" of the Apple. You'll get the principles, the playbooks, and the practical tools you can apply immediately.
No theory-only fluff. Just real results from real businesses scaling with intention.
And before we close, you'll learn how to align it all: your team, systems, KPIs, and growth strategy, into one cohesive engine built to scale.

WHY BUSINESSES STAY STUCK

There's a difference between being busy and being in control.

Too many business owners confuse momentum with progress. They mistake chaos for growth. They celebrate full calendars but ignore broken processes. And somewhere along the way, they realize: **I've built something I can't walk away from.**

Scaling isn't just about more revenue. It's about more freedom. More impact. More options.

But that only happens when you shift from being the **doer**... to being the **designer**.

WHAT YOU'LL LEARN (AND DO)

In this book, you'll learn how to:

- Hire and build teams that lead, not just follow
- Set up processes that duplicate your best people (starting with you)
- Create KPIs and accountability structures that drive performance
- Master execution and eliminate the "hero" syndrome
- Lead with clarity and make better, faster decisions
- Scale without burnout and stop reinventing the wheel

You'll also get:

- Plug-and-play frameworks
- Diagrams you can share with your team
- Stories from the trenches (both wins and mistakes)
- Bonus tools like **The Priority Filter** to zero in on what actually moves the needle

This is a book about scaling smart, not just scaling fast.

WHO THIS IS FOR

If you're a founder, executive, team leader, or operator looking to:

- Escape the cycle of daily firefighting
- Build systems your team actually uses
- Grow your business without losing your mind

...then this book was built for you.

You don't need more complexity. You need **clarity**. **Structure. Focus. Execution.**

Let's slice into this thing and build a business that works for you so you're not stuck working for it.

SLICE ONE

BUILDING HIGH-PERFORMING TEAMS

The Core of Growth

Your business will never grow past the strength of your team. Period.

I don't care how good your product is, how much revenue you've stacked, or how hard you grind. If your team is disorganized, uncommitted, or misaligned, your ceiling is already set.

So let's break this down. "Building a team" isn't about bodies in chairs. It's not about hiring fast or plugging holes. This is about building alignment. Ownership. Leadership duplication.

It's about hiring with intention, structuring for performance, and developing people who don't just clock in but buy in.

If you're the only one thinking like an owner, you're not scaling. You're surviving.

WHY MOST TEAMS DON'T SCALE

Here's the trap I see over and over again, especially in small-to-mid-sized businesses:

- The owner hires fast because they're overwhelmed.
- They skip the clarity and hire for convenience.
- A few months in, they're fixing mistakes, re-explaining tasks, and wondering why nothing sticks.

Sound familiar?

That's not a team problem. That's a leadership problem. You didn't design for scale; you duct-taped for survival.

Let's flip that script.

HIGH-PERFORMING TEAMS ARE BUILT, NOT FOUND

I've seen this firsthand. One client hired six field workers in a month, and had to replace four of them within 90 days because they skipped clarity to move fast. (More on that in the Core File at the end of this slice.)

High-performing teams don't magically appear. They're not the result of "getting lucky with good people." They're the byproduct of intentional structure.

Here's what that looks like:

- **You hire for impact, not just experience.** You don't need someone who's done the job before. You need someone who wants to crush it here with your vision, in your system.

- **You make expectations unavoidable.** Clarity is your best friend. If your team's confused, it's not on them. It's on you.

- **You structure teams to reduce friction.** Communication flows up and down. Roles are clean. Ownership is obvious. And people are set up to win.

- **You develop from within.** Stop hoping the next leader walks in your door. Create them. Give stretch projects. Give feedback. Give visibility.

Give a damn.

CUT THE NOISE: CULTURE IS NOT VIBES

Culture isn't happy hour. It's not bean bags. It's not a Spotify playlist. Culture is what your team does when you're not in the room.

- It's whether they double-check the client's invoice before sending.
- It's whether they step up or shut down when things go sideways.
- It's how they treat each other under pressure.

You don't "have" a culture. You build one. And the culture you build will either accelerate your growth or silently sabotage it.

THE 3 LEVELS OF TEAM ALIGNMENT

Let's make this tactical. High-growth companies align their teams across three levels:

1. HIRING FOR ALIGNMENT

- Are you screening for values, not just resumes?
- Do you have a documented hiring process with

consistent scorecards?

- Are your new hires walking into clarity or confusion?

2. STRUCTURING FOR OWNERSHIP

- Who owns what? Is that clear on paper or just in your head?
- Can people in your org make decisions without checking with you every time?
- Do your job descriptions connect to results?

3. DEVELOPING INTERNAL LEADERS

- Are you creating a leadership pipeline or just hoping the "right" person emerges?
- Are you giving feedback that actually develops someone or just venting?
- Are you measuring by output or by title?

THE 5-STEP TEAM BUILD FRAMEWORK

Let's make this actionable. If you're building or rebuilding your team, start here:

1. CLARIFY YOUR VISION

What are you building? Why does it matter?

Example: "We're building the most respected commercial construction firm in the region known for delivering on time, every time. That means every hire, every process, and every client touchpoint has to reflect precision, professionalism, and pride."

2. DEFINE OUTCOMES FOR EVERY SEAT

Not tasks. Outcomes.

Example: Instead of "answer the phone," a receptionist's outcome might be: "Deliver a five-star first impression and route calls within 60 seconds to the right person 95% of the time."

3. USE A CONSISTENT HIRING SYSTEM

Scorecards, interview templates, onboarding tracks.

Example: Use a position scorecard that ranks candidates 1–5 on culture fit, communication, and role-specific competencies. Then onboard with a 30-60-90 day plan tied to their scorecard metrics.

4. CREATE A FEEDBACK LOOP

Weekly check-ins, quarterly reviews, real-time adjustments. *Example:*

- Every Monday: 15-minute 1:1 with each direct report to align on goals
- Quarterly: Scorecard review and recalibration
- In between: Real-time shout-outs and course corrections

5. BUILD LEADERS, NOT JUST MANAGERS

Give responsibility. Coach consistently. Celebrate wins. *Example*: Have your ops lead run the weekly team meeting and present KPIs. Coach them through feedback sessions, decision-making, and handling conflict. When they hit goals, recognize it in front of the team.

COMMON PITFALLS

Here's what trips up most operators:

- Hiring from desperation instead of strategy
- Assuming people "get it" without repeating yourself 10 times

- Waiting too long to fix a poor fit
- Confusing loyalty with performance
- Believing leadership is "intuitive"? It's not. It's a skill, and it must be taught.

THE CORE FILES: BREAKING THE BOTTLENECK TO SCALE A $6M CONSTRUCTION FIRM

Industry: Specialty Construction
Revenue: $6M
Employees: 35

INITIAL CHALLENGE:

The owner was overwhelmed and deeply embedded in daily operations. Despite strong sales and job bookings, team performance was inconsistent, mistakes were frequent, and new hires didn't stick.

WHAT BROKE WHEN THEY SCALED:

As revenue climbed, so did rework, field confusion, and internal frustration. Hiring was done reactively to fill roles fast, but without scorecards, onboarding plans, or clear outcomes. The team relied on the owner for every decision, making her the bottleneck for scale.

THE SYMPTOMS:

- Repeated onboarding failures
- Team "loyalty" masking low performance

- No clear job descriptions or role KPIs
- Owner solving problems in real-time instead of building systems

THE APPLE EFFECT IN ACTION:

1. **Clarified the Vision**
   → "We build with precision, not chaos." That became the internal mantra.

2. **Defined Outcomes by Role**
   → Every seat had an outcome, not just a task list. (e.g., "Submit permit packets within 48 hours of contract close")

3. **Installed a Hiring Scorecard & 90 Day Ramp Up Plan**
   → Culture fit, technical ability, communication style

4. **Built a Weekly 1:1 Rhythm**
   → Team members reported before being asked; trust and accountability grew.

5. **Promoted from Within with Coaching Support**
   → A high-potential field lead was elevated into a team lead role with defined metrics and weekly feedback.

THE OUTCOME:

- $1.1M in revenue added in 6 months, without increasing headcount
- Turnover dropped from 35% to 10%
- The owner began stepping out of day-to-day decision making
- Weekly team meetings shifted from updates to ownership

THE STRATEGIC EDGE:

"You don't scale by doing more. You scale by duplicating clarity, leadership, and structure at every level."

SLICE ONE BITE-SIZED BIT

Your business is only as scalable as your team is strong. You don't grow by doing more; you grow by duplicating leadership, clarity, and ownership at every level.

"A thriving business starts with an aligned, accountable team. When you build the right culture, you build the right results."

IMPLEMENT THIS NOW

- Clarify your company's 3-year vision and share it with your team.
- Define outcomes, not tasks, for 3 core roles.
- Create and use a scorecard during every hiring

process.

- Schedule weekly 1:1s with direct reports.

- Promote one internal team member into a stretch leadership role.

IF YOU SKIP THIS

You'll stay the most capable person in the room, and the most overworked. Without structure and clarity, you're just duct-taping your way to burnout.

SLICE ONE NOTES & REFLECTIONS

Where are you hiring for convenience instead of performance? What's one role or person you need to redefine, re-align, or re-train for real impact?

_____
_____
_____
_____
_____
_____
_____
_____
_____
_____

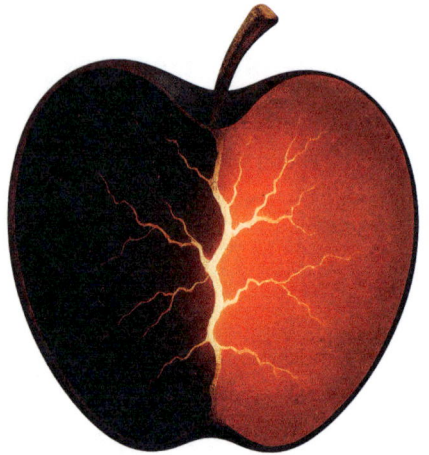

SLICE Two

CREATING ACCOUNTABILITY & OWNERSHIP AT EVERY LEVEL

Own the Outcome or Own the Excuse

Culture is your foundation, but without accountability, that foundation cracks under pressure.

You've seen how to build high-performing teams. Now, let's talk about getting every single person to act like they own the outcome, because culture alone won't carry the weight of scale; ownership will.

YOU CAN'T SCALE WHAT NOBODY OWNS

I've seen businesses lose deals, drop balls, and bleed revenue, not because the team didn't care, but because nobody was clearly, visibly, undeniably responsible.

Let's get this straight:

- **Accountability is not micromanagement.**
- **Ownership is not blame.**

This chapter is about building a culture where your team doesn't just do the job. They **own the result.**

One company I worked with missed a $12K invoice because everyone thought someone else was handling it. That moment changed everything for their accountability structure. You'll see how that played out in the Core File later in this slice.

THE BOTTLENECK TRAP

Every time I work with a business that's stuck, I ask one question: **"If something goes wrong here, who takes responsibility?"**

The answer is usually… crickets.

Why? Because too many owners are holding the reins too tight, or worse, they're unclear about who owns what.

When ownership isn't defined, it defaults back to you. That's how you become the bottleneck. That's how your 9-figure dreams get buried under $9 tasks.

Let's fix that.

WHY ACCOUNTABILITY GETS A BAD RAP

Too often, business owners avoid accountability conversations because they confuse them with confrontation. They don't want to "make it awkward" or "hurt someone's feelings."

But here's the truth: **Lack of accountability doesn't protect people, it sets them up to fail.**

And you know what? Top performers *want* to be held accountable.

- They want to know what winning looks like.
- They want the scoreboard. The clarity. The challenge.

It's not about micromanaging. It's about removing ambiguity and giving your team a clear runway to perform.

THE 3 LEVELS OF OWNERSHIP

Let's break down how real accountability is built across three distinct levels in your business:

1. SELF-ACCOUNTABILITY

- Each team member knows their metrics and what success looks like.
- They don't wait to be told. They report before you ask.
- They ask themselves, "*Did I do what I said I would do?*"

2. PEER ACCOUNTABILITY

- Teams hold each other to standards.
- They follow through out of respect, not just compliance.
- Meetings aren't just check-ins. They're commitment reviews.

3. LEADERSHIP ACCOUNTABILITY

- Managers model what they expect.

- Leaders don't hide from hard conversations. They lean into them.
- Expectations are documented, measured, and reinforced consistently.

Ownership is a muscle. And muscles only grow under pressure.

THE ACCOUNTABILITY FRAMEWORK

Use this structure when defining roles and responsibilities inside your business. If it's vague, it's not scalable.

ACCOUNTABILITY COMPONENT BREAKDOWN

- **What:** *What is the outcome or result this person is accountable for?*
- **When:** *What is the timeline or cadence (daily, weekly, quarterly)?*
- **How:** *How will this be measured or reported?*
- **Who:** *Who is ultimately responsible, and do they know it?*

Run this for every critical outcome in your business. If you can't answer all four, **ownership is not clear.**

THE ACCOUNTABILITY CONVERSATION

Want to handle underperformance without drama? Here's the script:

"I want you to win. But part of winning here means owning your results. Here's what was expected. Here's what happened. Can you help me understand the gap?"

Then listen.

"What do you need to hit the mark next time?" "What's the consequence if this continues?"

You're not scolding. You're clarifying. You're not punishing. You're protecting the team's standards. Because what you tolerate becomes your culture.

COMMON MISTAKES

Let's call out the five accountability killers I see most:

- **Vague expectations:** "Own the client experience" means nothing without specifics.

- **No follow-up rhythm:** One-time goals with no check-ins = dead goals.

- **Fear of confrontation:** If you won't address performance, your top players will leave.

- **Overlapping roles:** If three people own it, no one does.

- **No scoreboard or KPI:** People need to know if they're winning or just working.

PRO TIP: USE A WEEKLY OWNERSHIP REVIEW (END-OF-WEEK REPORT)

This is a simple email format I give to my clients. Each team member shares:

- "Here's what I committed to last week."

- "Here's what I accomplished."

- "Here's what I'm committing to this week."

No gray area. Just consistent, clear, and confident ownership.

THE CORE FILES: THE $12K MISTAKE, AND THE SHIFT TO OWNERSHIP

Industry: Custom Residential Construction
Revenue: $4.8M
Team Size: 25

INITIAL CHALLENGE:

The company was growing fast, but accountability was lagging. A $12K billing error went unnoticed until a client flagged it. No one knew who was supposed to catch it. "That's not my job" became a common phrase.

WHAT BROKE WHEN THEY SCALED:

As departments expanded, responsibilities blurred. Change orders were logged late. Invoices were delayed. Projects slowed. When issues surfaced, the team scrambled, but didn't solve the root cause.

THE SYMPTOMS:

- No one took responsibility unless asked directly
- Team relied on the owner or PMs to follow up on everything

- Scorecards weren't being reviewed, or didn't exist

- Excuses sounded like, "I thought Kasey had that," or "I didn't see the email"

THE APPLE EFFECT IN ACTION:

1. **Installed Ownership Anchors**
   → Every critical task got a single owner (not a group)

2. **Introduced End-of-Week Reports**
   → Each team member submitted 3 bullets:

   ○ What I committed to

   ○ What I accomplished

   ○ What I'm committing to next week

3. **Created a Weekly KPI Rhythm**
   → Lagging issues (like revenue delays) were tied to leading indicators (like invoice submission timing)

4. **Trained Managers on the Accountability Conversation**
   → We roleplayed tough conversations: "I want you to win. But winning means owning the result."

5. **Documented the Accountability Framework**
   → What / When / How / Who applied to every role

THE OUTCOME:

- Invoicing delays dropped by 60%
- Change order approval time reduced by 3 days
- 100% of team members now submit weekly ownership reports
- "It wasn't me" turned into "That's on me, and here's my plan to fix it"

THE STRATEGIC EDGE:

"Accountability isn't confrontation, it's alignment. When every outcome has an owner, nothing slips through the cracks."

SLICE TWO BITE-SIZED BIT

If no one owns the outcome, no one owns the success. Accountability isn't punishment. It's alignment. Ownership doesn't restrict freedom. It **unlocks** it.

When everyone owns their lane, your business accelerates without you pushing every pedal.

IMPLEMENT THIS NOW

- Assign one clear owner for every critical outcome.

- Roll out weekly end-of-week reports to the team.

- Document the What / When / How / Who for each key process.

- Train managers on how to deliver accountability conversations with clarity and care.

- Link role scorecards to at least one measurable KPI.

IF YOU SKIP THIS

Tasks will drift. Accountability will blur. And results will depend on how loudly you yell instead of how clearly you lead.

SLICE TWO NOTES & REFLECTIONS

What critical outcome in your business still lacks a clear owner? What's one area where "it's not my job" is costing you time, money, or trust, and what will you do to fix it?

_____
_____
_____
_____
_____
_____
_____
_____
_____
_____
_____

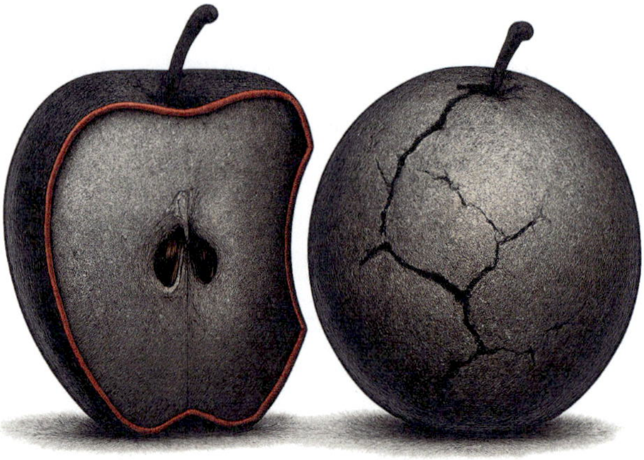

SLICE
Three

APPLES & ORANGES

Why Copying What Works for Others Can Break What You're Building

When everyone starts thinking like an owner, the next temptation is to look around and copy what the "big players" are doing.

Don't fall for it.

In this chapter, we're going to dismantle the dangerous myth that what worked for them will work for you. This is where the **Apple vs. Orange Matrix** comes in.

SAME INDUSTRY, DIFFERENT FRUIT

Just because it *looks* like the same business doesn't mean it *works* the same. It's like comparing apples to oranges.

And people do it in business all the time. They look at a competitor's revenue, team size, fancy CRM setup, or number of Instagram followers and start spiraling:

"Why aren't we there yet?" "Shouldn't we be doing that, too?" "What are we missing?"

Let me save you a few years and a few thousand dollars:

You're not behind. You're just different.

In fact, if you try to scale your business by copying someone else's fruit basket, you'll probably break the very thing that makes you great.

THE COMPARISON TRAP

Comparison without context is one of the fastest ways to destroy momentum.

Why? Because you start making decisions from insecurity instead of insight.

Here's the deal:

- You can't scale what you don't understand.
- You can't optimize what wasn't built for duplication.
- And you *definitely* can't outperform a company whose model, team, and systems you don't fully grasp.

Trying to mimic another business without knowing their backend is like trying to build a Ferrari by looking at the paint job.

I had a client hit $10M in revenue, but they copied a competitor's playbook and ended up with broken ops and zero margin growth. That case taught them the cost of imitation. (You'll see it unpacked in the Core File at the end.)

APPLES GROW IN ORCHARDS. ORANGES GROW IN GROVES.

Let's break it down.

You may see two companies generating $5M in revenue. But one is powered by documented SOPs, trained teams, and systematized service delivery. The other? Running on the CEO's charisma, a few hero employees, and pure adrenaline.

They both taste sweet on the outside, but only one can multiply.

And here's the kicker: Even comparing yourself to your *past self* can be misleading.

What worked at $1M might actually hurt you at $5M, especially if you haven't rebuilt your structure to support the scale.

STRATEGY CHECK: IS YOUR BUSINESS BUILT TO DUPLICATE?

Run this internal test. Ask yourself:

- If I doubled my client load tomorrow, could my systems handle it?
- If I stepped away for a week, would results stay the same or drop?
- Am I making decisions based on where I'm going or where I've been?

If you can't confidently answer "yes" to all three...You're still building for quick wins when what you need is a model that **multiplies**.

THE APPLE VS. ORANGE MATRIX

BUSINESS ELEMENT: STRUCTURE

The Apple (Scalable Business): SOPs, defined roles, accountability, repeatable processes
The Orange (Non-Scalable Business): Undefined roles, tribal knowledge

BUSINESS ELEMENT: REVENUE ENGINE

The Apple: Systems drive sales
The Orange: Hustle drives sales

BUSINESS ELEMENT: TECH USE

The Apple: Enhances throughput & reporting
The Orange: Band-aid for chaos

BUSINESS ELEMENT: GROWTH STRATEGY

The Apple: Duplicates leaders, trains systems
The Orange: Adds headcount, throws bodies at problems

BUSINESS ELEMENT: LEADERSHIP TIME

The Apple: Spends time *on* the business
The Orange: Spends time *in* the business

JUST BECAUSE IT WORKED DOESN'T MEAN IT SCALES

Your hustle got you here, but it won't get you there.

This chapter isn't a warning against ambition. It's a reminder that your **structure** has to match your **vision**.

You don't need more motivation. You need more mechanics.

So stop mimicking. Start engineering.

Because at the end of the day, it's not about whether your business *looks* like someone else's.

It's about whether it can *outlast* them.

THE CORE FILES: THE $10M COPYCAT TRAP

Industry: Manufacturing & Install
Revenue: $10M
Employees: 50

INITIAL CHALLENGE:

The owner had big ambition, and was modeling the business after a top competitor with slick branding, a national reach, and fast growth. They rushed to implement similar CRM tools, pricing models, and marketing language, but performance stalled.

WHAT BROKE WHEN THEY SCALED:

They were copying the "front of house" without the back-end mechanics. The flashy CRM went unused. New services were sold before the ops team could fulfill them. Culture declined, margins shrank, and burnout surged.

THE SYMPTOMS:

- Constant tool-switching with no adoption
- Sales outpaced fulfillment capacity
- Increased rework, missed deadlines, and deliv-

ery errors

- Frustration from the ops team: "We can't keep up with the promises sales is making."

THE APPLE EFFECT IN ACTION:

1. **Ran the Strategy Check**
   → Asked: "If you doubled your client load tomorrow, would your systems hold?"
   → Answer: "No. They'd collapse."

2. **Used the Apple vs. Orange Matrix**
   → Compared their business structure, tech use, and throughput capacity against the competitor's, but from the inside-out

3. **Shifted Focus to Duplication, Not Imitation**
   → Paused expansion and re-invested in internal SOPs, throughput tracking, and training loops

4. **Rebuilt the Org Chart Around Accountability**
   → Clear lanes for Sales, Ops, and Fulfillment with a visual tracker for project flow

5. **Implemented "Earn the Add-On" Rules**
   → No new service launches without 90 days of execution margin greater than 30%

THE OUTCOME:

- 23% increase in gross margin in 90 days
- $750K saved in operational inefficiencies
- Culture rebuilt through clarity, not hype
- Competitor envy replaced with confidence in their own systems

THE STRATEGIC EDGE:

"You don't scale by mimicking someone else's playbook. You scale by building a business that can actually multiply."

SLICE THREE BITE-SIZED BIT

You don't scale by copying someone else's fruit basket. You scale by **engineering a model built to multiply**.

What looks like success on the outside might be running on hustle, not systems. Stop chasing someone else's model. Start designing. **Build what works for *your* business.**

IMPLEMENT THIS NOW

- Run the Strategy Check on your current business model.

- Use the Apple vs. Orange Matrix to evaluate your operations, tech, and revenue engine.

- Pause any new initiative that isn't backed by a

duplicable system.

- Define what makes your business unique, and engineer scale around that.

- Stop comparing. Start building.

IF YOU SKIP THIS

You'll waste time copying someone else's model, and break what actually makes you great.

SLICE THREE NOTES & REFLECTIONS

Where have you been tempted to copy another business's strategy without checking if your model can support it? What makes your business uniquely scalable, and how will you double down on that instead?

_____
_____
_____
_____
_____
_____
_____
_____
_____
_____

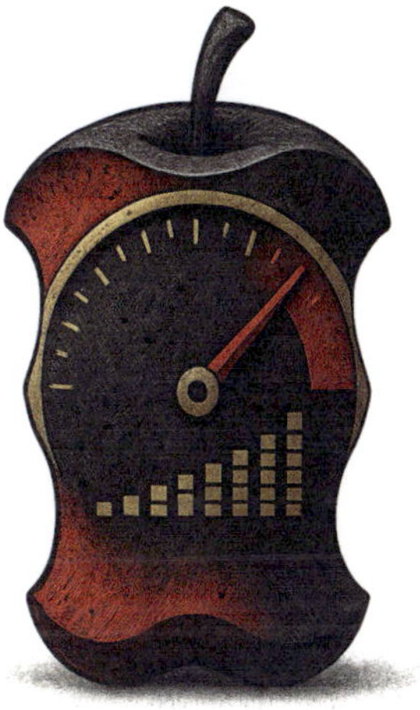

SLICE Four

KPI MASTERY

Turning Data into Scalable Decisions

Now that you've seen how comparisons can cost you clarity, it's time to trade guesswork for precision. You can't scale on vibes; you scale on visibility.

Let's dive into KPIs and learn how to make smarter, faster decisions using numbers that actually move the business.

IF YOU CAN'T MEASURE IT, YOU CAN'T GROW IT

Worse? If you're measuring the wrong things, you'll scale in the wrong direction or not at all.

This chapter isn't about stuffing your dashboards with a hundred numbers no one looks at. It's about building the **right scoreboard**. One that drives clarity, accountability, and predictable growth.

KPI MASTERY IN ACTION: ACTIVITY VS. THROUGHPUT

KPI TYPE: ACTIVITY

- **Measures:** Hours worked
- **What It Helps You See:** Input / Effort

KPI TYPE: THROUGHPUT

- **Measures:** Days to completion
- **What It Helps You See:** Output / Speed of delivery

KPI TYPE: COMBINED VIEW

- **Measures:** Hours + Days
- **What It Helps You See:** Efficiency & Scalability

Takeaway: You don't grow by working harder. You grow by completing more, faster, **without sacrificing quality**.

So ask yourself: Are you measuring **motion**... or **momentum**?

DATA DOESN'T LIE, BUT YOU MIGHT NOT BE LISTENING

I see it all the time:

- Leaders making gut calls
- Teams celebrating busyness, not outcomes
- Dashboards that collect dust

When KPIs aren't part of the culture, here's what happens:

- Sales slows down and no one knows why
- Customer complaints pile up with no pattern recognition
- A-players go unrecognized while underperformers fly under the radar

KPI mastery closes that gap. It's how you move from **reactive** to **predictive**.

One business tracked everything *except* what mattered. They were "on budget", but bleeding margin quietly every month. When we shifted their KPI focus, we found a 6-point margin swing. You'll see that full breakdown in the Core File.

THROUGHPUT: YOUR SCALING SUPERPOWER

Before you track everything, track what's slowing you down.

Throughput shows how many clients or projects can successfully flow through your business each week without overwhelming your team or disappointing your customers.

The red bar is your bottleneck. Until that stage improves, your entire business is capped no matter how strong the rest is.

KPI Mastery = Using data to unlock flow, not just track performance.

KPI VS. METRIC: KNOW THE DIFFERENCE

Not all numbers are created equal.

- A **metric** is just a number.
- A **KPI** is a number that moves your business.

KPI = Directly tied to revenue, retention, efficiency, or growth. If it doesn't move the needle, it's a distraction.

KPI VS. METRIC

KPI: Sales conversion rate
Metric: Website traffic

KPI: Gross margin %
Metric: Vendor count

KPI: Customer retention
Metric: Instagram likes

KPI: Jobs completed on time
Metric: Slack messages sent

Your team can track metrics. **You lead with KPIs.**

THE 3-TIER KPI STRUCTURE

- **Company-Level KPIs** Your North Star. Measures health and drives strategy. *Examples: Revenue, EBITDA, Client Retention*

- **Department-Level KPIs** Align each department to the mission. *Examples: Close rate (Sales), Project cycle time (Ops)*

- **Role-Level KPIs** Individual ownership. Every number connects to the next level. *Example:* "Permits submitted within 5 business days"

This is how you build a culture of ownership. Everyone knows their number. Every number serves the mission.

LEADING VS. LAGGING INDICATORS

Indicator Type: Lagging
What It Tells You: What already happened
Examples: Revenue, Churn, Profit

Indicator Type: Leading
What It Tells You: What's coming
Examples: Sales calls, Proposals

Lagging = Scoreboard

Leading = Playbook

You need both, but **leading helps you steer the ship.**

THE KPI FEEDBACK LOOP

KPIs should evolve. They're not carved in stone.

Keep them alive by following this rhythm:

1. **Define**: Tie to a goal. Be specific.

2. **Assign**: One clear owner per KPI.

3. **Track**: Weekly check-ins, live dashboards

4. **Adjust**: Ask: Are these still the right KPIs?

5. **Communicate**: KPIs should show up in every meeting

KPIs are only powerful when they're part of the conversation.

COMMON KPI MISTAKES

Here's how KPI systems break down:

- Tracking too many (pick 3–5 per role, not 30)
- Overweighting lagging metrics
- No ownership
- Vanity metrics over valuable ones
- Ignoring red flags until it's too late

You don't need more data. **You need better direction.**

WEEKLY KPI REVIEW: REAL-WORLD RHYTHM

Here's how to bring KPI accountability to life.

Weekly Check-In Format:

- What was your KPI target?

- What was your actual?
- What worked?
- What didn't?
- What's your plan to improve?

This rhythm builds consistency. It creates visibility. It transforms performance from **mystery to mastery**.

THE CORE FILES: THE INVISIBLE MARGIN LEAK

Industry: Commercial Construction
Revenue: $7.5M
Employees: 40

INITIAL CHALLENGE:

The business was growing in top-line revenue, but margin was slowly eroding. Projects were "on time" but rarely on profit. The team tracked hours and job completion, but not throughput or efficiency.

WHAT BROKE WHEN THEY SCALED:

They celebrated busyness instead of outcomes. Labor hours were logged, materials ordered, and jobs closed, but actual profit on each project was unknown until well after the fact. By the time issues were caught, it was too late to recover margin.

THE SYMPTOMS:

- No visibility into actual job cycle time
- PMs overwhelmed and reactive
- Monthly financials showed profit drops but lacked cause

- "On budget" jobs were actually leaking cash due to slow completions

THE APPLE EFFECT IN ACTION:

1. **Installed KPI Tiering (Company Dept Role)**
   → Made sure every KPI rolled up and down with clarity and ownership

2. **Tracked Throughput, Not Just Activity**
   → Added "Planned vs. Actual Completion Days" to dashboard
   → This immediately revealed execution drag, even when hours looked fine

3. **Built a Weekly KPI Review Cadence**
   → Each role owned 3–5 KPIs, reported weekly (target vs. actual), and shared one action to improve

4. **Simplified Dashboards to Show What Matters**
   → Replaced 22 "vanity metrics" with 7 KPIs tied to revenue, margin, or execution

5. **Reinforced Leading Indicators**
   → Sales: Quotes sent
   → Ops: Project kickoff timelines
   → Admin: Invoicing within 3 days of closeout

THE OUTCOME:

- Project completion improved by 32%
- Margin per job increased by 6.8 points
- The owner no longer had to micromanage job health. KPIs told the story
- Culture shifted from reactive to data-driven

THE STRATEGIC EDGE:

"You scale on visibility. And every role should know exactly what number they own."

SLICE FOUR BITE-SIZED BIT

You don't scale with spreadsheets. You scale with **scoreboards**. KPIs turn chaos into clarity. They predict problems. They spotlight progress. And most importantly, they give your team a **number they can own**.

When your team owns their number, **they own their outcome**.

IMPLEMENT THIS NOW

- Choose 3 company-level KPIs that truly drive revenue, margin, or retention.

- Assign 3–5 KPIs to each department and role.

- Launch a weekly KPI check-in rhythm: Target,

Actual, Plan to Improve.

- Replace vanity metrics with throughput-based KPIs.

- Build a shared KPI dashboard visible to your whole team.

IF YOU SKIP THIS

You'll confuse activity with progress, and stay blind to the performance patterns that could scale or sink your business.

SLICE FOUR NOTES & REFLECTIONS

Which KPI in your business is missing, misaligned, or misunderstood? What's one number you need your team to own starting this week to unlock better decisions and faster growth?

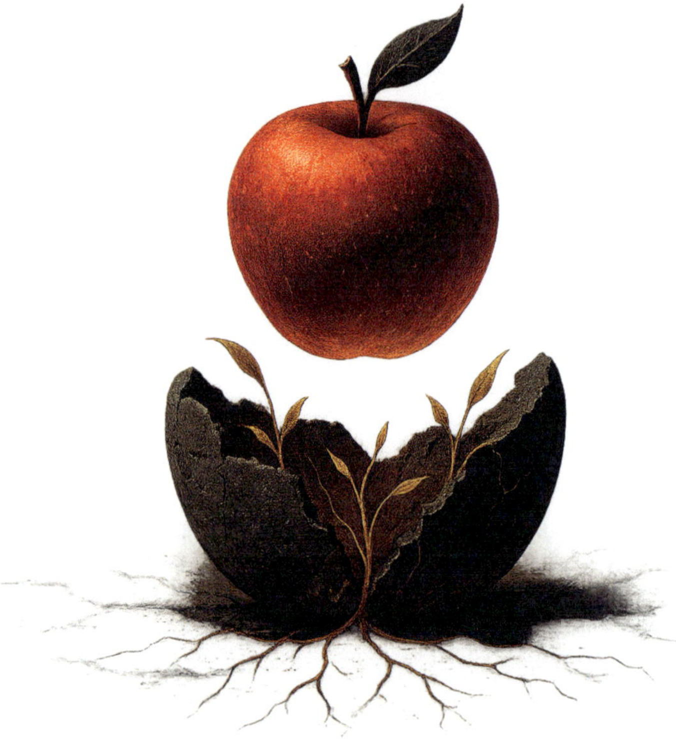

SLICE FIVE

THE GROWTH MINDSET

Scaling Beyond Comfort Zones

Data gives you confidence, but **it's your mindset that determines how far you're willing to go**.

If you want different results, you need different thinking. Let's talk about the uncomfortable but necessary shift from playing it safe... to playing for scale.

YOUR COMPANY WILL NEVER GROW BIGGER THAN YOUR MINDSET ALLOWS

If you're playing it safe, avoiding discomfort, or waiting for "the right time" to push, guess what?

You're already the ceiling.

Every business I've helped scale beyond $5M, $10M, $25M had one common trait:

The owner was willing to outgrow their habits, beliefs, and comfort zones.

This chapter isn't surface-level hype. This is a **strategic wake-up call**.

If you want next-level results, it starts with **next-level thinking**.

I worked with a founder who knew how to hustle, but not how to lead with belief. His team mirrored his fear until we rewired the culture. The shift started with mindset, and you'll see how it changed the game in the Core File at the end.

FIXED MINDSET = STALLED BUSINESS

Let's define the enemy.

A FIXED MINDSET IS WHEN YOU:

- Avoid taking risks unless success is guaranteed
- Resist feedback or feel personally attacked by it
- Stick with what works, even if it's not scalable

- Make excuses for stagnation by blaming "the market," "the team," or "the industry"

Sound familiar? Fixed mindset doesn't show up all at once. It creeps in quietly under the disguise of "being realistic."

And that's exactly how businesses plateau.

GROWTH MINDSET = SCALABLE IDENTITY

Now let's flip it.

A GROWTH MINDSET IS WHEN YOU:

- See problems as puzzles, not threats
- Ask better questions instead of defaulting to blame
- Embrace feedback as fuel
- Play for the long game, even when short-term pain shows up

Here's the deal: **Your business is a reflection of your beliefs.**

If you don't believe in the potential of your team, your model, or your leadership, it will show. And it will shape every decision you make.

Scaling isn't just tactical. It's psychological.

YOUR MINDSET SETS THE CULTURE

Whatever mindset you carry... **multiplies**.

- If you overreact to problems, so will your team.
- If you're scarcity-minded, so are your managers.
- If you avoid accountability, your entire org will start hiding.

Culture doesn't follow your words. It follows your weather.

You've got to be the **thermostat**, not the **thermometer**. You set the tone. You anchor the confidence. You model resilience.

That's how growth becomes contagious.

REAL EXAMPLE - MINDSET IN ACTION:

• A $2.5M service company was stuck. The founder avoided delegating because past hires had failed.

• We introduced a "test and trust" model, delegating one major responsibility with clear KPIs.

- Within 60 days, the team member exceeded expectations, and the founder shifted from control to coaching.

- That single mindset shift unlocked two new hires and $500K in added revenue within the quarter.

3 BELIEFS THAT SCALE

There are three core mindset beliefs I see in the most successful leaders:

1. **"Everything is figureoutable."** They don't spiral. They strategize. They don't panic. They plan.

2. **"My success is tied to my willingness to change."** They understand that what got them here won't get them there.

3. **"Failure is feedback."** Instead of hiding from mistakes, they mine them for data, process gaps, and leadership lessons.

When these beliefs become your default operating system, your business can't help but grow.

THE IDENTITY SHIFT OF A SCALING CEO

Let's get personal.

The most painful growth stage is when you have to shift from:

"I'm the expert who solves it all" → "I'm the leader who builds the people who solve it all."

That's not easy. Your ego will fight it. Your habits will resist it.

But it's the only way to grow past being "just the person who does it best."

SCALING REQUIRES:

- Duplication
- Delegation
- Trust
- Feedback

And none of that works if you're stuck clinging to your comfort zone.

CLIENT STORY: MINDSET SHIFT, REVENUE LIFT

A landscape company in California was stuck at $2M. He had the people. He had the product. But he couldn't crack the next level.

The bottleneck? **Mindset. His and his team's.**

He used to tell his crew:

"Clients look out the window and check the cameras to see what you're doing. Don't mess up."

It was fear-based. It kept the team small, careful, and reactive.

Then he flipped the script:

"Clients are watching, so show off. Be great. Let them see the caliber and care of this team."

That one shift changed everything.

It wasn't just better morale. It was **ownership**. It was **pride**. It was **performance**.

And it showed up in the numbers:

The company went from $2M to $4M shortly after, driven by increased upsells, referrals, and repeat business.

That's the power of mindset. When leadership believes, the team delivers.

PRACTICAL STEPS TO BUILD A GROWTH MINDSET CULTURE

HERE'S HOW TO OPERATIONALIZE MINDSET ACROSS YOUR ORG:

- **Normalize feedback.** Make it regular. Make it safe. Make it two-way.
- **Celebrate effort and evolution, not just wins.** Recognize people who take initiative, even if the result isn't perfect.
- **Challenge fixed beliefs in meetings.** Ask: "What are we assuming here that might not be true?"
- **Use failure debriefs.** After every missed goal, ask: "What worked? What didn't? What would we do differently next time?"
- **Reinforce learning as part of the job.** Invest in coaching, training, and reflection.

THE CORE FILES: FROM FEAR-BASED TO FUTURE-FOCUSED

Industry: Multi-Trade Construction (Plumbing, Tree, Fence)
Revenue: $3.2M
Employees: 18

INITIAL CHALLENGE:

The founder was holding everything together by force of will, making every decision, solving every problem, and shouldering the stress of multiple verticals. He knew growth was possible… but didn't trust the team to carry it forward.

WHAT BROKE WHEN THEY SCALED:

The owner hit decision fatigue. His instinct was to slow down expansion and "tighten control" rather than delegate. The result? Missed sales opportunities, overwhelmed field staff, and rising turnover.

THE SYMPTOMS:

- Fear of delegation
- No internal promotions due to "no one being

ready"

- High-potential team members disengaged
- Owner stuck in a reactive loop of small decisions

THE APPLE EFFECT IN ACTION:

1. **Challenged the Fixed Beliefs**
   → "No one can do it like me" became: "What would happen if they could, with support?"

2. **Introduced Weekly Leadership Coaching**
   → Focused on mindset shifts: feedback, ownership, and confidence-building

3. **Promoted One Emerging Leader with Guardrails**
   → Gave a team member control of a vertical, with weekly metrics and a support rhythm

4. **Celebrated Growth Behaviors, Not Just Wins**
   → Publicly recognized problem-solving, initiative, and leadership, not just results

5. **Reframed Mistakes as Feedback**
   → Each "miss" became a lesson: What worked? What didn't? What will we try differently next time?

THE OUTCOME:

- The owner stepped back from day-to-day management in one vertical
- The promoted leader increased vertical revenue by 27% in 90 days
- Team engagement rose visibly, and recruiting got easier
- The owner now hosts a monthly leadership roundtable instead of solving daily problems

THE STRATEGIC EDGE:

"Your business will never outgrow your mindset. When you shift from fear-based control to growth-based coaching, everything changes."

SLICE FIVE BITE-SIZED BIT

You don't grow by playing it safe. You grow by playing it **smart** and staying **uncomfortable**.

A growth mindset doesn't mean you ignore problems. It means you believe in your ability to solve them.

When your mindset scales, your business follows.

IMPLEMENT THIS NOW

- Identify one fear or hesitation holding you back, then take action anyway.
- Shift your self-talk: "Failure is feedback."
- Lead one meeting this week with a growth-mindset prompt: "What did we learn?

What would we try differently?"

- Give praise for effort and initiative, not just outcomes.

- Ask your team: "What uncomfortable action would move us forward fastest?"

IF YOU SKIP THIS

Your business will inherit your hesitation. Culture won't grow. And the discomfort you're avoiding will become the ceiling you can't break.

SLICE FIVE NOTES & REFLECTIONS

What would you do differently if you believed your next level required a mindset upgrade? What's one uncomfortable action you've been avoiding that would unlock serious momentum if you took it today?

_____
_____
_____
_____
_____
_____
_____
_____
_____
_____
_____

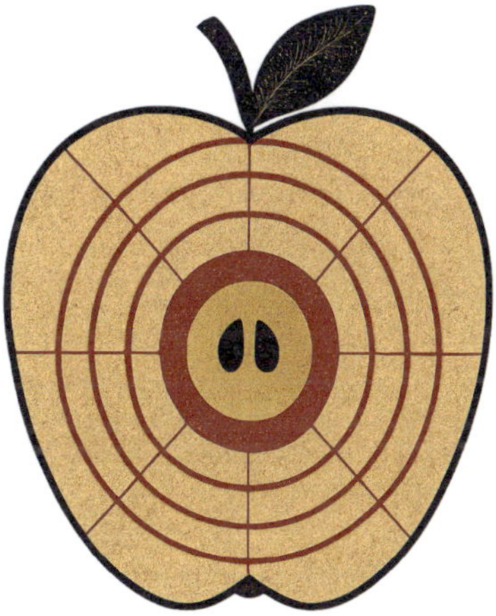

SLICE SIX

MASTERING OKRS & PERFORMANCE ALIGNMENT

Clarity. Focus. Momentum.

Once you've leveled up your mindset, it's time to align your goals with your team's daily actions. No more New Year's resolution-style goals that vanish by Q2.

In this next slice, we'll turn growth into a system using OKRs so your results aren't just inspiring… **they're inevitable.**

IF YOUR TEAM ISN'T ROWING IN THE SAME DIRECTION…

Your business isn't scaling. It's **burning fuel**.

One of the biggest reasons companies stall after $3M, $5M, or even $10M is simple:

They confuse **activity** with **alignment**.

Everyone's "busy", but are they busy doing the right things?

Is every project, task, and initiative moving the company toward its targets?

If the answer is "kind of" or "I think so," lean into this chapter.

Let's lock in the tool high-growth businesses use to align at every level: **OKRs**.

WHAT ARE OKRS?

OKR = Objectives and Key Results

They answer two critical questions:

- **What are we trying to accomplish?** (Objective)
- **How will we know we're making progress?**

(Key Results)

Simple? Yes. Easy to implement? Not without intention. Worth it? **100%**.

OKRS VS. KPIS

Before we go further, let's clear up the confusion.

KPIS

- Ongoing performance indicators
- Tell you how a function is performing
- Typically stable
- Maintain stability

OKRS

- Short-term goals with measurable outcomes
- Tell you what you're trying to achieve
- Reset quarterly or by project
- Drive transformation

Here's the move: You **run** the business on KPIs. You **grow** the business with OKRs.

WHY OKRS MATTER FOR SCALE

WITHOUT OKRS, COMPANIES FALL INTO CHAOS:

- Priorities shift weekly
- Projects lose momentum
- Teams operate in silos
- Managers get reactive, not strategic

WITH OKRS:

- Focus is locked in across every level
- Leaders are clear on what matters most
- Execution speeds up
- Everyone knows what "done" looks like

OKRs are the alignment engine that connects daily actions to business outcomes.

One 90-person company I worked with had vision, but no alignment. Their departments were spinning in different directions until we installed OKRs that synced every action to results. That transformation is detailed in the Core File that follows.

ANATOMY OF AN OKR

OBJECTIVE (THE WHAT)

- Clear, inspiring, and directional
- Focuses on an **outcome**, not activity
- Example: "Improve our sales process to increase close rate"

KEY RESULTS (THE HOW WE'LL KNOW)

- 2–5 per Objective
- Specific, measurable, and time-bound
- Drive behavior and progress
- Examples:
  - "Increase sales call-to-close ratio from 18% to 25% by Q2"
  - "Reduce average sales cycle time from 22 to 15 days"

Each Key Result is a **milestone**. Hit them, and the Objective becomes reality.

HOW TO BUILD OKRS THAT WORK

Here's the 5-step process I use with clients:

1. **Start with your company vision:** What must happen this quarter to move closer?
2. **Set 3–5 high-leverage Objectives:** Don't overwhelm your team. Prioritize what matters.
3. **Build measurable Key Results:** If it can't be measured, it's not a Key Result.
4. **Assign clear owners:** Every OKR must have **one person accountable**, even if others support.
5. **Check progress weekly:** Visibility creates accountability. No "surprises."

EXAMPLES BY FUNCTION

SALES

Objective: Increase average deal size

- KR1: Raise avg. deal value from $18K to $24K by June 30
- KR2: Launch bundled pricing for 3 core services

OPERATIONS

Objective: Improve client onboarding speed

- KR1: Cut onboarding time from 12 to 7 days
- KR2: Launch onboarding checklist with SOPs by May 1

MARKETING

Objective: Boost lead quality from paid ads

- KR1: Increase MQL-to-SQL conversion rate to 35%
- KR2: Launch 3 new landing pages with clear CTAs

HUMAN RESOURCES

Objective: Improve leadership team performance

- KR1: Conduct 360 reviews for all department heads by end of Q2
- KR2: Launch leadership training curriculum by July 15

COMMON OKR MISTAKES

Let's save you the heartache. Here's where most businesses get it wrong:

- **Too many Objectives** – Limit to 3–5 max per org/department

- **Vague Key Results** – "Improve service" is not a Key Result

- **No weekly rhythm** – OKRs not reviewed weekly get forgotten

- **No owner = no outcome** – Assign ownership, or don't bother

- **Misaligned goals** – Department OKRs must tie to company goals

THE ALIGNMENT FLOW

This is how OKRs should cascade:

- **Company-Level OKRs:** Vision-aligned, revenue-driving, and quarterly reset

- **Department OKRs:** Translate company objectives into function-specific goals

- **Individual OKRs:** Tie directly to role KPIs and

project execution

When alignment is this tight, you create **unstoppable momentum.**

THE LEADERSHIP CHALLENGE

Setting OKRs isn't a checkbox exercise. It's a **leadership discipline.**

You must ask:

- Are we aligned?
- Are we tracking?
- Are we adjusting based on data?
- Are we reinforcing these goals in every meeting, check-in, and dashboard?

You don't just **set** OKRs. You **lead through them.**

THE CORE FILES: FROM CHAOS TO CADENCE

Industry: Systems Integration & Field Services
Revenue: $18M
Employees: 90+ across departments

INITIAL CHALLENGE:

The leadership team had a strong vision, but that vision wasn't translating into aligned, measurable action. Teams were "busy" but not coordinated. Marketing, operations, and sales were all rowing in different directions.

WHAT BROKE WHEN THEY SCALED:

Without a clear goal framework, each department defaulted to firefighting. Projects started fast and fizzled. Accountability slipped. Department heads were reactive, not strategic.

THE SYMPTOMS:

- No clear company-wide quarterly goals
- Projects drifted without measurable results
- Weekly meetings felt like status updates, not performance check-ins

- Department leads couldn't articulate what "winning this quarter" meant

THE APPLE EFFECT IN ACTION:

1. **Facilitated a Cross-Department OKR Sprint**
   → Created 3 company-wide Objectives with supporting Key Results

2. **Cascaded OKRs Down to Department + Role Level**
   → Every department lead had 2–3 OKRs aligned with the company goals
   → Individual contributors linked their weekly tasks to a Key Result

3. **Installed a Weekly OKR Review Rhythm**
   → Each team shared wins, blockers, and percent-to-target on Key Results

4. **Made OKRs Visual**
   → Live dashboards showed progress in real time; leaders led with metrics, not motion

5. **Paired OKRs with Accountability Conversations**
   → Weekly check-ins included: "Where are we stuck?" and "What's the next best move?"

THE OUTCOME:

- Weekly focus aligned across all departments for the first time
- Projects completed 22% faster due to fewer priority shifts
- Leadership team moved from reacting to orchestrating
- Sales and Ops teams finally shared a common scoreboard

THE STRATEGIC EDGE:

"Momentum isn't built by doing more. It's built by syncing your team to the outcomes that count. When your OKRs drive daily action, momentum becomes inevitable."

SLICE SIX BITE-SIZED BIT

You don't scale by trying harder. You scale by **aligning better**.

OKRs give your business:

- Clarity on where you're going

- Focus on what matters now

- Visibility on what's working (and what's not)

If KPIs are your pulse, **OKRs are your pace.**

Let's make sure every part of your business is moving in the same direction. With purpose and power.

IMPLEMENT THIS NOW

- Set 3 company-wide Objectives with 2–3 measurable Key Results each.

- Assign a clear owner to each OKR (not a team).

- Roll out department and individual OKRs tied to company targets.

- Use a simple Google Sheet or dashboard for weekly OKR tracking.

- Host a weekly 15-minute OKR review per team.

IF YOU SKIP THIS

Your team will stay "busy" but misaligned. And your quarterly goals will drift into next year without a fight.

SLICE SIX NOTES & REFLECTIONS

Is your team busy or aligned? What's one objective that's critical to your growth this quarter and how will you ensure every team member connects their work to it?

_____
_____
_____
_____
_____
_____
_____
_____
_____
_____
_____

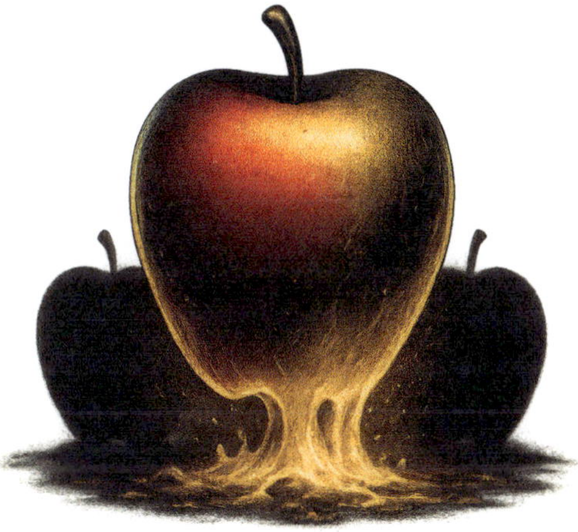

SLICE SEVEN

MASTERING LEADERSHIP

Leading for Growth & Scale

Setting the right goals is one thing. **Leading people to hit them?** That's where things get impactful.

This chapter is about shifting from being **"the doer"** to becoming **"the duplicator."** It's about leading in a way that builds people, not just solves problems.

Because you're not building a business to run forever. You're building a business that can run without you.

YOU DON'T SCALE BY DOING MORE. YOU SCALE BY LEADING DIFFERENTLY

You can be the most skilled operator, the best closer, or the smartest strategist...But if your leadership doesn't evolve, your business won't either.

Boss vs. Leader: Know the Difference

Let's draw the line:

BOSS VS. LEADER

BOSS

- Tells people what to do
- Solves every problem
- Seeks control
- Delegates tasks
- Focuses on power

LEADER

- Inspires people to think critically
- Coaches others to solve and grow
- Builds trust
- Delegates outcomes
- Focuses on multiplying performance

If you're still the hero, the firefighter, the fixer, then your team doesn't have a leader. They have **you**… doing it all.

But that's not leadership. That's a liability. And it's not scalable. Not sustainable. Not how you build a business that outgrows you.

THE CONTROL TRAP

One of the hardest shifts for founders is letting go of control.

WHY?

- Because you know how to do it "right"
- Because trusting others feels risky
- Because you've been burned before

But here's the truth: **If you're involved in every decision, you've built a dependency. Not a business.**

Control feels like confidence. But it's often just fear dressed up as process.

Real leadership is about empowerment. Multiplication. Replication. Accountability.

FIELD STORY - THE COST OF CONTROL:

- A construction owner reviewed every invoice personally, even though he had a finance lead.

- When he finally delegated the task with clear expectations and a 24-hour turnaround policy, errors dropped.

- More importantly, the finance lead gained confidence and started spotting margin risks proactively.

- The owner reclaimed 6 hours per week and started using that time to mentor his PMs instead of triaging admin.

THE LEADERSHIP MULTIPLICATION FRAMEWORK

Here's how I coach leaders to scale themselves beyond their own capacity:

1. **Document what only you know.** If your best work lives in your brain or inbox, it's a liability. Start building processes.

2. **Define what success looks like.** Clear expectations. Metrics. Outcomes. No guessing.

3. **Delegate with ownership.** Don't hand off tasks. Hand off **targets**. Let people build their own

path to the result.

4. **Coach weekly.** Feedback isn't a quarterly event. It's a rhythm. A pulse. A culture.

5. **Create visibility.** Scoreboards. Dashboards. Reviews. People can't improve what they can't see.

This is how you build **leaders** inside your company, not just task-doers.

THE 3 TRAITS OF SCALABLE LEADERS

Want to grow your leadership (and your company) fast? Develop these:

1. **Clarity:** Communicate the why, the what, and the win. Remove ambiguity and align on outcomes.

2. **Consistency:** Your team should know what to expect from you every week. If your leadership is reactive, your culture will be too.

3. **Coaching:** Great leaders don't just correct. They **develop**. They ask better questions. They build future leaders, not just current performers.

REAL EXAMPLE: FROM OPERATOR TO SCALER

I worked with a business owner stuck around $3M. She was running ops, solving every issue, reviewing every invoice, leading every team meeting.

She didn't have a **leadership problem**. She had a **duplication problem**.

WE STARTED WITH HER CALENDAR:

- Stripped out $10 tasks
- Built a leadership team with clear KPIs
- Created a weekly coaching cadence

WITHIN 6 MONTHS:

- She was out of the weeds
- Her department heads were owning their roles
- The business is now on track to hit $5M this year

Because when you scale your leadership, **you scale everything**.

THE LEADERSHIP ALIGNMENT FRAMEWORK

Use this to assess and align your leadership team right now:

LEADERSHIP ACCOUNTABILITY CHECK

Ask yourself the following questions and answer **Yes or No** honestly:

- Does each leader own a clear outcome?
- Are they reviewing KPIs weekly?
- Do they coach their teams consistently?
- Can they run their function without you?
- Do they develop others or just delegate tasks?

Got more "No" than "Yes"? Don't panic. Just get to work.

HOW TO BUILD LEADERS INSIDE YOUR ORG

- **Promote based on performance and potential.** Not just tenure. Who thinks like an owner?
- **Train the new expectation of leadership.** Leading isn't just doing. It's enabling, influenc-

ing, and measuring.

- **Mentor with metrics.** Set development KPIs for your leaders: retention, team performance, cultural strength.

- **Create shadowing and stretch assignments.** Let future leaders earn their seats by solving bigger problems.

THE CORE FILES: THE HERO TRAP

Industry: General Contracting
Revenue: $6.5M
Employees: 30+

INITIAL CHALLENGE:

The owner was the smartest person in the room, and the busiest. He was solving issues across bids, client calls, permits, field ops, and invoicing. His team admired him. But they didn't grow. And it was burning him out.

WHAT BROKE WHEN THEY SCALED:

The owner became the bottleneck. The team waited for his approval. New hires mimicked his hustle but couldn't replicate his decisions. Leadership was defined by presence, not performance.

THE SYMPTOMS:

- Everyone defaulted to "Ask [Owner]"
- Promising employees plateaued
- No one else ran team meetings or held 1:1s

- Projects stalled if the owner was out

THE APPLE EFFECT IN ACTION:

1. **Mapped Time vs. Value**
   → We reviewed the owner's weekly calendar and flagged every $10/hour task he was doing.

2. **Delegated Outcomes, Not Tasks**
   → Team leads took ownership of revenue-driving outcomes (e.g., bid follow-up close rate)

3. **Promoted a PM into Leadership, with Guardrails**
   → Gave them visibility, stretch goals, and KPIs, plus coaching on hard conversations

4. **Trained Leaders to Run the Meetings**
   → They now open meetings, review KPIs, and coach others using a weekly rhythm

5. **Created a Leadership Scorecard**
   → Measured each leader on: team performance, retention, and coaching cadence

THE OUTCOME:

- The owner cut 12 hours a week from operations
- Leadership depth increased, 2 people now run

revenue meetings

- Internal promotion pipeline formed for the first time
- The business moved from personality-based to performance-based

THE STRATEGIC EDGE:

"Leadership isn't what you do, it's what you duplicate. When you build leaders, your business stops relying on your presence and starts growing through your people."

SLICE SEVEN BITE-SIZED BIT

If you want to scale your business, **scale your leadership.**

Your role isn't to do it all. Your role is to **build the people who do it well.**

When your team can think, act, and lead with clarity, you're no longer the engine. **You're the architect.**

That's scalable leadership.

IMPLEMENT THIS NOW

- Audit your calendar: delegate any task under your pay grade.
- Promote one team member and coach them weekly for 90 days.
- Define and assign outcome ownership, not just task lists.
- Create a leadership scorecard: KPIs, retention, feedback cadence.
- Let another leader run the next team meeting, then debrief together.

IF YOU SKIP THIS

You'll stay stuck as the "hero" instead of the builder. And when you go down, the business follows.

SLICE SEVEN NOTES & REFLECTIONS

Where are you still solving problems instead of building the people who solve them? What's one leadership behavior you can duplicate in your team starting this week?

_____
_____
_____
_____
_____
_____
_____
_____
_____
_____
_____

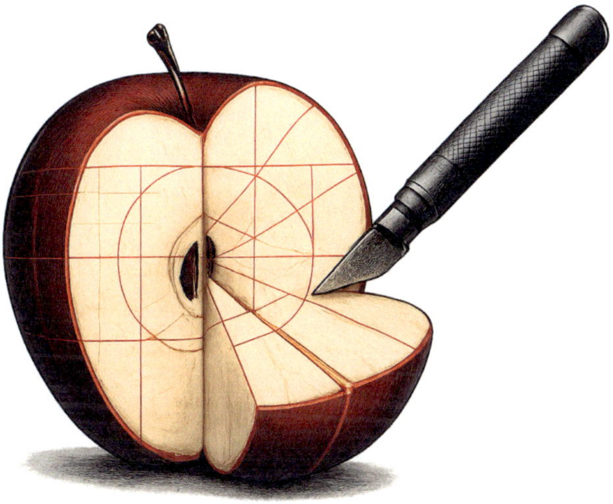

SLICE
Eight

PRECISION EXECUTION

Turning Action into Momentum

Great leadership sets the vision, but execution turns vision into reality. This is where the rubber meets the road.

In this final slice, we'll map out how to drive momentum every single week through process, precision, and action.

BUSY DOESN'T BUILD. EXECUTION DOES.

There's a reason businesses with less talent, fewer resources, and smaller teams still outrun the competition:

They know how to **execute with precision**.

They don't just get things done. They get the **right things** done on time, on target, with intention.

THIS CHAPTER IS ABOUT MOVING FROM:

- Activity → **Traction**
- Chaos → **Clarity**
- "Always working" → **Actually winning**

Scaling is about doing what matters, and doing it well.

THE MYTH OF HARD WORK

We've been sold the lie that hustle is enough.

But the graveyard of burned-out businesses is filled with hard-working people who never stopped long enough to build a system that worked without them.

What you execute consistently is what scales.

If it only works when you're in the room, it's not a system. It's a stress loop.

Let's fix that.

WHAT PRECISION EXECUTION LOOKS LIKE

Companies that scale consistently share five execution traits:

- Clear priorities
- Defined processes
- Structured follow-through
- Accountability baked into every action
- Simplicity in how work moves through the business

It's not exciting. It's not flashy. **But it's powerful.**

Execution is what turns ideas into income. It's what transforms strategy into success.

WHAT HAPPENS WITHOUT EXECUTION DISCIPLINE

On the flip side, businesses that lack execution discipline:

- Start fast and fizzle out
- Launch ideas without follow-through
- Create SOPs no one reads

- Say "yes" to everything and finish nothing
- Lose trust with clients and employees

Lack of execution is a leadership issue. A process issue. A follow-up issue. A focus issue.

THE EXECUTION ENGINE: HOW TO BUILD IT

Here's how I help clients **operationalize execution**:

1. **Define the Outcome:** Don't assign tasks. Assign results. Everyone should know what "done right" looks like.

2. **Document the Process:** Process = repeatability. If you've done it more than twice, write it down.

3. **Assign Ownership:** One person. One deliverable. One timeline. Shared responsibility = no responsibility.

4. **Install a Tracker:** Use a visible dashboard or scorecard. Weekly reviews. No guessing.

5. **Close the Loop:** Follow-up is not micromanagement. It's leadership.

ASK:

1. Was it done?

2. Was it done right?

3. What's next?

PRECISION PROCESS TRACKING

I teach every client to use a **Process Navigator.** A single source of truth.

It answers three questions:

- What's the process?
- Who owns it?
- When was it last updated?

A Process Navigator removes chaos. It ensures SOPs are real, followed, and effective.

The less you have to repeat, the more you can scale.

USE THE PRIORITY FILTER

If everything feels urgent, nothing is.

Here's my 3-question filter to prioritize execution:

1. **Does it directly impact revenue, margin, or retention?** If yes, this is a priority.

2. **If the person responsible quit today, would it break?** If yes, document immediately.

3. **If duplicated, would it increase output without hiring?** If yes, this has scale leverage.

If the answer is "yes" to two or more, it's a **Priority**. Lock it in. Document it. Build around it.

EXECUTION CULTURE CHECKLIST

Here's how you know if your team is built for precision:

- People know the outcomes they own
- You have documented processes for repeatable tasks
- There's a rhythm of accountability (weekly reviews, scoreboards, trackers)
- The team knows how to prioritize when time or resources are tight
- "Done" means "done right," not just "checked off"

If this list feels aspirational, good. Now you know what to build.

EXECUTION KILLERS TO ELIMINATE

Let's name them so we can crush them:

- **Vague delegation** – "Can you handle this?" (No.)
- **Unclear timelines** – "Get to it when you can." (It won't.)
- **Lack of follow-up** – "Let me know how it goes." (You'll never hear back.)
- **Overcomplicated systems** – "Click here, then open that, then export this…" (No one will do it.)

Execution dies in confusion. **Simplicity scales.**

THE CORE FILES: THE 20-HOUR FIX

Industry: Precast Manufacturing & Installation
Revenue: $8.2M
Employees: 45

INITIAL CHALLENGE:

The owner was spending nearly 20 hours per week chasing mistakes, clarifying expectations, and reassigning tasks. Despite having good people, nothing stuck. SOPs were loose. Priorities shifted daily. "Done" didn't always mean "done right."

WHAT BROKE WHEN THEY SCALED:

As volume increased, execution buckled. Missed deadlines. Field reloads. Lost time. Every team was working, but no one was working in sync. Everyone blamed "the process," but there wasn't one to follow.

THE SYMPTOMS:

- Constant rework in the yard and field
- No single source of truth for key tasks
- Leaders unsure who owned what or when it was due

- Owner buried in daily problem-solving

THE APPLE EFFECT IN ACTION:

1. **Mapped the Execution Engine**
   → Defined five traits of scalable execution: clarity, process, ownership, tracking, and follow-up

2. **Created a Process Navigator**
   → A live, centralized SOP dashboard showing who owns what, how it's done, and when it was last updated

3. **Implemented a Priority Filter**
   → Every task reviewed against:
   - Revenue or margin impact
   - System fragility
   - Scale potential

4. **Assigned Ownership for Every Step**
   → One person per task. No "shared" responsibility. Each line item had a name next to it.

5. **Launched a Weekly Execution Review**
   → Each lead shared updates on 3 priorities: On track / Off track / Action needed

THE OUTCOME:

- Rework in the field dropped by 40%
- The owner got back 20 hours/week, without hiring
- SOPs became living documents, not dusty PDFs
- Teams aligned around what mattered most, and executed faster

THE STRATEGIC EDGE:

"Execution is about doing the right things, the right way, with the right follow-up. That's how you scale without stress."

SLICE EIGHT BITE-SIZED BIT

Great businesses don't just have ideas. They **execute them like machines**.

Precision execution gives you:

- Time freedom
- Team confidence
- Client trust
- Revenue consistency

You don't need more time. **You need more systems.**

When execution is locked in, you stop carrying the business, and start scaling it.

IMPLEMENT THIS NOW

- Define the outcome, not the task, for every project in motion.

- Create a single-source Process Navigator with ownership and SOP links.

- Implement The Priority Filter across your team's project list.

- Host a weekly Execution Review with team leads: On Track / Off Track / Needs Action.

- Track and publish 3 throughput KPIs weekly.

IF YOU SKIP THIS

You'll keep spinning in chaos and calling it growth. Execution isn't optional, it's the machine your business runs on.

SLICE EIGHT NOTES & REFLECTIONS

Where is "almost done" or "done-ish" hurting your growth? What's one SOP, tracker, or follow-up system you can install to ensure execution happens with precision not guesswork?

_____
_____
_____
_____
_____
_____
_____
_____
_____
_____
_____

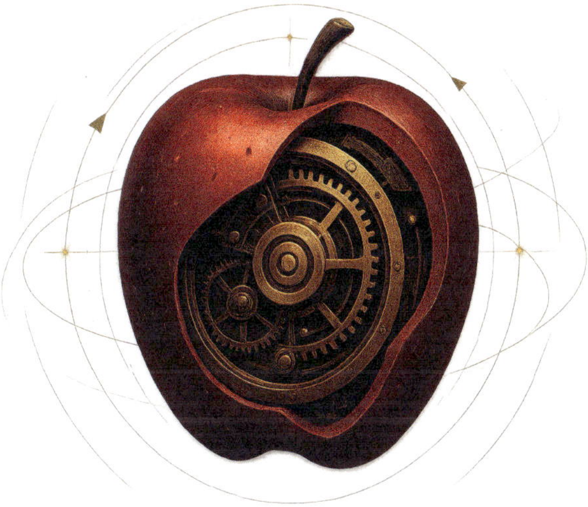

THE C.O.R.E. STRATEGY ENGINE

Engineered to Scale. Built to Last.

L et's strip it down to what really moves the needle.

You've seen how to build teams, install systems, track KPIs, drive accountability, and lead for scale. Here's what most business books gloss over:

All of that dies in the absence of strategy.

When I say strategy, I'm talking about the engine that aligns every part of your business with revenue, margin, retention, and replicable performance.

This is the strategy that makes scale predictable and not accidental.

And it's built right into the C.O.R.E.

WHY MOST STRATEGY FAILS

Because it lives on a deck.
Or it lives in your head.
Or worse, it lives nowhere at all.

Most business owners are running on reaction and not intention. They chase growth without engineering it. They think strategy is something you visit once a year, not something you operationalize every week.

That's why growth feels reactive instead of intentional.

THE C.O.R.E. AS A STRATEGIC OPERATING SYSTEM

Let's revisit the framework, this time as your strategic engine.

- Culture & Teams
- Operational Excellence
- Results & Accountability
- Expansion & Innovation

It's not just a framework. It's how you think, plan, and execute. It's how you scale without breaking.

So let's make it tactical.

THE C.O.R.E. STRATEGY STACK

This is the blueprint I use with high-growth clients to align execution with impact.

1. CULTURE DRIVES HIRING AND RETENTION STRATEGY

Strategic Question:
Who do we need to win the next stage of growth, and are we building them now?

Action Step:
Define your 3-year team structure. Then reverse-engineer the leadership pipeline.

If You Skip This:
You'll keep hiring reactively and wonder why you're always managing chaos.

2. OPERATIONS DRIVE EFFICIENCY AND MARGIN STRATEGY

Strategic Question:
Where are we losing time, money, or trust? Is it documented or delegated?

Action Step:
Pick your top 3 revenue-impacting processes. Document them. Assign ownership. Measure throughput.

If You Skip This:
Scale will magnify your inefficiencies instead of your impact.

3. RESULTS DRIVE KPI AND ACCOUNTABILITY STRATEGY

Strategic Question:
What do we measure, and does it actually move the business forward?

Action Step:
Rebuild your scorecard. One KPI per role, tied directly to revenue, margin, or retention. Weekly reporting.

If You Skip This:
You'll stay busy but misaligned. Performance will be a guessing game.

4. EXPANSION DRIVES MARKET AND INNOVATION STRATEGY

Strategic Question:
Are we scaling what's proven or chasing what's shiny?

Action Step:
Audit your offerings. 80/20 your pipeline. Only scale what's duplicable, profitable, and predictable.

If You Skip This:
You'll grow in circles instead of forward.

THE C.O.R.E. STRATEGY FLYWHEEL

This isn't a checklist. It's a flywheel. Each piece drives the next and builds unstoppable momentum.

WHEN YOU LOCK THESE FOUR IN ALIGNMENT, HERE'S WHAT HAPPENS:

- Culture gives you the right people.
- Operations give them the right tools.
- Results give you the right scoreboard.
- Expansion gives you the right direction.

Round and round. Faster and faster. With less of you required at every turn.

That's real strategy and how legacy is built.

C.O.R.E. STRATEGY SNAPSHOT

Before you see this in action, pause and assess where your business stands right now.

USE THIS ONCE PER QUARTER TO SHARPEN YOUR EDGE:

C.O.R.E Element: Culture
Strategic Focus: Leadership pipeline
What Needs to Shift: _____
_____
_____

C.O.R.E Element: Operations
Strategic Focus: Process efficiency
What Needs to Shift: _____
_____
_____

C.O.R.E Element: Results
Strategic Focus: KPI visibility
What Needs to Shift: _____
_____
_____

C.O.R.E Element: Expansion
Strategic Focus: Product or market leverage
What Needs to Shift: _____
_____
_____

Don't overthink it. Use this to ask better questions and make sharper decisions.

THE CORE FILES: FROM STALLED TO STRATEGIC

Industry: Industrial Services
Revenue: $14M
Employees: 62

INITIAL CHALLENGE:

The leadership team was burned out. Growth had stalled. The CEO was still in every meeting, solving every problem. Strategy lived in their head but didn't survive past Monday.

Teams were busy but disconnected. Every department had a different version of what mattered. Priorities shifted. Projects stalled. The company wasn't broken, but it wasn't built to scale.

WHAT BROKE WHEN THEY SCALED:

With growth came complexity, not clarity.
Siloed execution. KPIs no one owned. Missed margin goals.
The ops team blamed sales. Sales blamed fulfillment. The CEO became the bridge between everything. Burnout took the wheel.

THE SYMPTOMS:

- Department leads operating without a shared scoreboard
- Projects started, then fizzled with no measurable outcomes
- Quarterly goals felt "nice to have" instead of non-negotiable
- CEO stuck in the weeds instead of steering strategy

THE APPLE EFFECT IN ACTION:

1. **Facilitated a Strategic Realignment Sprint**
   → Built 3 company-wide Objectives with measurable Key Results tied to growth targets

2. **Cascaded the C.O.R.E. Strategy Stack into Department Plans**
   → Each department created its own C.O.R.E. -aligned initiatives based on company goals

3. **Installed KPI Visibility and Weekly Tracking**
   → Weekly rhythm of Target vs. Actual reviews with owners and outcomes

4. **Defined the "Revenue 3" Processes**

→ Focused documentation and throughput tracking on their highest-margin workflows

5. **Rebuilt the Leadership Pipeline**
   → Promoted 2 internal leaders with coaching, metrics, and clearly defined outcomes

THE OUTCOME:

- Revenue increased by 18% in 6 months
- Net margin climbed 6 points
- CEO exited day-to-day meetings within 90 days
- Every department now connects weekly work to company strategy

THE STRATEGIC EDGE:

"You don't scale by doing more. You scale by aligning strategy, execution, and ownership with intention."

THE C.O.R.E. BITE-SIZED BIT

You scale not just by setting goals.
You scale by aligning people, process, metrics, and direction with intention.

Strategy isn't what you write. It's what you reinforce, track, and replicate.

IMPLEMENT THIS NOW

- Print the C.O.R.E. Strategy Snapshot and complete it with your leadership team.

- Identify the weakest C.O.R.E. quadrant in your business today. Focus your next 30 days there.

- Launch a weekly strategy huddle. 20 minutes. Ask:

- What's our priority?
- What's the blocker?
- Who owns the outcome?
- How do we measure success?

IF YOU SKIP THIS

You'll keep doing more and wonder why you're not getting better. You'll grow by effort instead of by design. You'll stay the bottleneck, and strategy will stay a theory.

CORE NOTES & REFLECTIONS

Which C.O.R.E. quadrant is driving your business right now, and which is dragging it? What's one strategic shift you've been avoiding because it felt too big, too complex, or too unfamiliar? Write it down. Then make the first move. One strategic decision can unjam the entire machine.

_____
_____
_____
_____
_____
_____
_____
_____
_____
_____

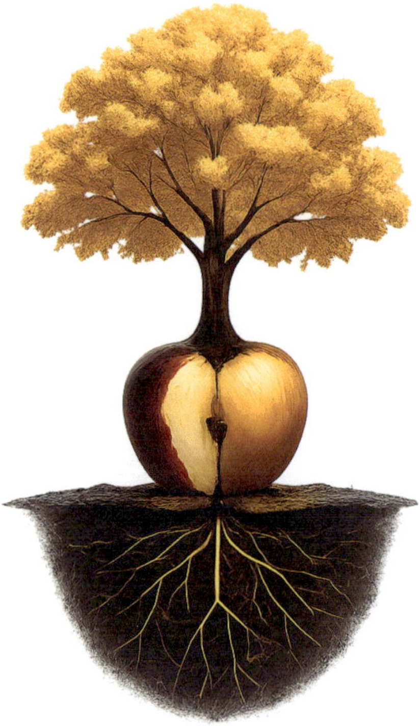

THE WHOLE: WRAPPING IT ALL TOGETHER

BUILDING A LEGACY BUSINESS

You've built your C.O.R.E. You've seen how to hire with intention, lead with clarity, drive accountability, and engineer strategy that scales. But none of it matters if you stay stuck in the weeds.

The final chapter is your shift from **operator to architect** because building a legacy business requires more than just doing the work. It takes designing a machine that works without you.

YOU'VE MADE IT THROUGH EVERY SLICE

You've dug into **strategy**, **systems**, **structure**, and **scale**. Now it's time to bring it all home.

Let's recap what *The Apple Effect* gave you and where you go from here.

FROM C.O.R.E TO MOMENTUM

EVERYTHING WE'VE COVERED MAPS BACK TO YOUR C.O.R.E.:

- **Culture & Teams** → Hire, build, and lead A-players who scale with you

- **Operational Excellence** → Document, delegate, and drive consistency

- **Results & Accountability** → Measure what matters and align your team to it

- **Expansion & Innovation** → Lead through growth, stay future-focused, and leverage what works

If you build from the core, your business becomes **durable**. If you neglect the core, your business becomes **fragile**.

This is your blueprint.

FROM VISION TO EXECUTION

YOU NOW HAVE:

- A hiring framework to build high-performing teams

- A system for creating extreme ownership
- Tools to measure what matters and eliminate distractions
- A method to align your company around powerful OKRs
- A leadership model that scales people, not just products
- An execution engine that multiplies your capacity

Don't wait to implement everything. Pick the slice that hit hardest, and take one messy, immediate step toward execution. Progress beats perfection. Movement beats overwhelm.

You don't need more tools or more ideas.

You need the **courage to act** on what you now know.

BUILDING A LEGACY

Scale is impressive. But **legacy** is transformational.

A LEGACY BUSINESS:

- Operates with clarity at every level

- Grows without drama or dependence on one person
- Develops leaders who multiply impact
- Creates value far beyond profit
- Leaves behind systems, culture, and standards that outlast the founder

FINAL THOUGHT: THE BUSINESS YOU DESERVE

You didn't read this book because you wanted another "feel-good" idea. You read it because you're **building something meaningful**.

And meaningful businesses aren't built off memory. They're built off **models**.

You've got the model now. You've got the frameworks. You've seen what's possible.

Now the real question is:

Will you execute it?

No one's coming to do it for you. Your team, your clients, your future, they're all waiting for you to lead this thing to the next level.

YOUR FINAL ACTION PLAN

HERE'S YOUR NEXT MOVE:

1. Pick the top 3 frameworks from this book that hit home hardest

2. Implement them in the next 30 days. **Imperfect but done**

3. Use **The Priority Filter** to decide what must be documented, delegated, or duplicated

4. Schedule a **quarterly C.O.R.E review** with your leadership team

5. Commit to becoming the leader who **scales through others, not around them**

YOUR LEGACY STARTS NOW

You don't need to be **bigger** to be better. You need to be **better** to go bigger.

You've now got the tools, the language, and the systems. Now go use them to build something **bold**, **profitable**, and **sustainable**.

Let *The Apple Effect* take root and grow a business that outlives your involvement, outpaces your competition, and outlasts the average.

You were never meant to carry it all. **You were meant to build it right.**

Let's go!

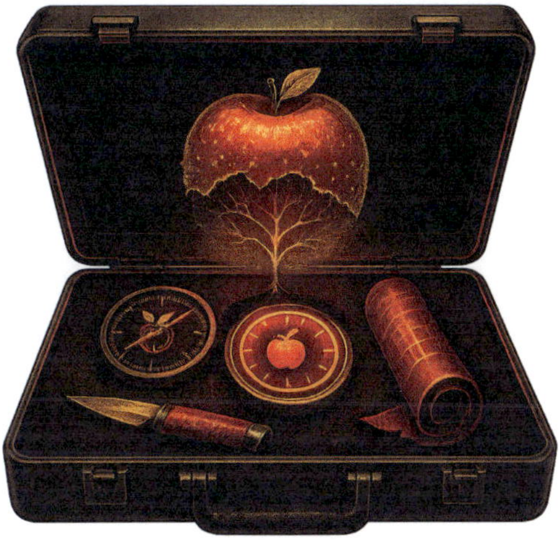

BONUS RESOURCE: THE C.O.R.E KIT

Tech & Templates to Implement Faster

Now that you know what to do, it's time to put it into action.

The C.O.R.E Kit is your shortcut. These are the tech tools, templates, and systems I use with clients every day. Think of it as your **scale-up toolbox**.

You made it through every slice of *The Apple Effect*. Now it's time to put it in motion, **fast**.

This bonus section is your tactical launch pad. These are the same tools and frameworks I've helped implement across dozens of companies, from startups to 8-figure industry leaders.

USE THIS KIT TO:

- Cut down implementation time

- Standardize your internal systems
- Multiply your results without multiplying your workload

SECTION 1: TECH STACK SETUP (BY FUNCTION)

Here's a simplified breakdown of the tools I recommend most often:

TOP TOOLS BY FUNCTION

FUNCTION: PROJECT MANAGEMENT

- **Top Tools to Start With:** ClickUp, Asana, Monday.com
- **This is Why It Works:** Clarity, timelines, cross-team visibility

FUNCTION: SOP DOCUMENTATION

- **Top Tools to Start With:** Trainual, Google Drive + Loom, YouTube
- **This is Why It Works:** Easy to scale. Easy to update. Easy to teach.

FUNCTION: KPI/OKR TRACKING

- **Top Tools to Start With:** Google Sheets
- **This is Why It Works:** Visual dashboards + accountability

FUNCTION: AUTOMATION

- **Top Tools to Start With:** Zapier, HubSpot
- **This is Why It Works:** Turns busywork into workflows

FUNCTION: INTERNAL COMMS

- **Top Tools to Start With:** Slack, Microsoft Teams
- **This is Why It Works:** Keeps ops moving without meetings

Pro tip: Don't use every tool. Start with one per function. **Simplicity scales.**

SECTION 2: TEMPLATES TO DEPLOY

SOP TEMPLATE – THE ACE MODEL

AIM: Define the purpose. *Why does this process matter?*

CLARITY: Set the standards. *What does "done right" look like?*

EXECUTION: Map the method. *What are the exact steps to follow?*

Add visual aids (screenshots, videos) and version tracking for extra impact.

KPI DASHBOARD TEMPLATE

TRACK WEEKLY:

- **Leading KPIs** – Calls made, deals quoted, tasks completed
- **Lagging KPIs** – Revenue, margin, client churn
- Owner | Target vs. Actual | Notes & Follow-Up

Visibility = Accountability = Performance

OKR PLANNING TEMPLATE

Use this format for every OKR:

OBJECTIVE: INCREASE SALES EFFICIENCY

- **Key Result 1:** Raise close rate from 20% to 30%
- **Key Result 2:** Reduce sales cycle by 5 days
- **Owner:** Jenna R.
- **Timeline:** Q2

Reset quarterly. Review weekly. Drive alignment.

WEEKLY TEAM REVIEW FORMAT

EVERY LEADER ANSWERS:

- What did I commit to last week?
- What was the result?
- What am I committing to this week?
- Where do I need support?

Use this to create a weekly rhythm that builds trust and execution culture.

ONBOARDING CHECKLIST (FIRST 30 DAYS)

FOR EVERY NEW HIRE:

- Tech setup complete
- Role overview delivered (with outcomes)
- SOP library access granted
- 3-Phase (30/60/90) goals reviewed
- Check-in cadence confirmed

First 30 days = foundation for performance.

SECTION 3: LEADERSHIP DEVELOPMENT CADENCE

MONTHLY LEADER DEVELOPMENT FORMAT:

- One leadership principle (communication, coaching, delegation)
- One roundtable: "*Where am I bottlenecking my team?*"
- One commitment: "*What will I implement this month?*"

You don't just grow leaders, you build a **culture of leadership**.

FINAL TIP: DON'T JUST DOWNLOAD. DEPLOY.

The fastest way to scale your company is to **systemize your thinking**.

START WITH:

- 1 SOP
- 1 KPI tracker
- 1 OKR
- 1 review rhythm

Then duplicate the results across every department. Scale with **clarity**.

THIS ISN'T THE END, IT'S YOUR LAUNCHPAD

TAKE WHAT YOU'VE BUILT IN THIS BOOK AND SCALE IT WITH:

- **Precision**
- **Purpose**
- **Power**

You've got the blueprint. You've got the tools. Now go build something that works with or without you.

Let's go get it!

ABOUT THE AUTHOR

Apple Levy is a bold performance strategist and advisor who transforms disorganized teams and systems into scalable, high-growth machines. With deep roots in operational leadership and a track record of scaling companies across construction, trades, and service-based industries, Apple brings a rare mix of real-world execution and strategic precision to every engagement.

As a trusted advisor to founders, CEOs, and leadership teams, she has helped scale businesses from $1M to $50M+ by aligning culture, systems, and accountability. Her frameworks are grounded in data but built to move people because she knows firsthand that sustainable growth starts with operational strength and duplicatable leadership.

Apple is a keynote speaker at business growth events and a recognized expert in team performance, KPIs, and execution systems. Her ability to simplify complexity, challenge complacency, and drive results has made her a sought-after voice in boardrooms and on stage.

If you're a founder who's ready to scale with clarity, build a team that owns the outcome, and stop being the bottleneck in your own business, Apple is the strategic partner you've been looking for. Her mission is simple: turn your vision into executable momentum and ensure you never outgrow your systems again.

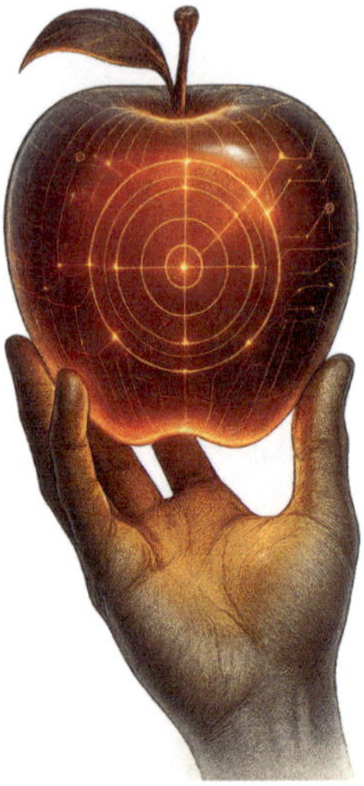

LET'S TAKE THE APPLE EFFECT OFF THE PAGE

AND INTO YOUR BUSINESS

You've got the blueprint. Now let's bring it to life.

If *The Apple Effect* gave you the clarity to think bigger and the tools to lead better, imagine what we could build together with hands-on strategy and support.

- Book Apple to speak at your next event
- Schedule a strategy session to scale your business
- Explore done-with-you consulting to implement the CORE frameworks

Visit **www.AppleLevy.com** or email **strategy@AppleLevy.com**.
Let's build a business that outlives your involvement and outperforms the average.

Made in the USA
Columbia, SC
02 July 2025

45dfe3a4-832c-4ab1-b1e5-8ac4e317508fR01